The Wolf Marshall Guitar Method

Primer

This primer is designed for the beginning student interested in the fundamentals of guitar playing, reading music, and getting a proper start. Included are etudes and pieces which have redeeming musical value in addition to simply presenting notes to read. By these means, a link between learning the basics and creating a playing repertoire is established early on in the guitarist's career. My teaching philosophy has always stressed a "hands on" approach for the student, striking a balance between theory and performance. This primer to the **Wolf Marshall Guitar Method** series is offered to aspiring guitarists everywhere as a vital first step.

Wolf Marshall

Now Available as Book Only, or Book/CD!

In the book/CD format, the accompanying recording contains 50 play-along tracks—including all the songs and etudes in this book. To find a track quickly, simply match its audio icon (◆) to the track number on your CD display.

HAL•LEONARD®

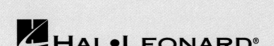

T0051124

Parts Of The Guitar

Electric Guitar

Acoustic Guitar

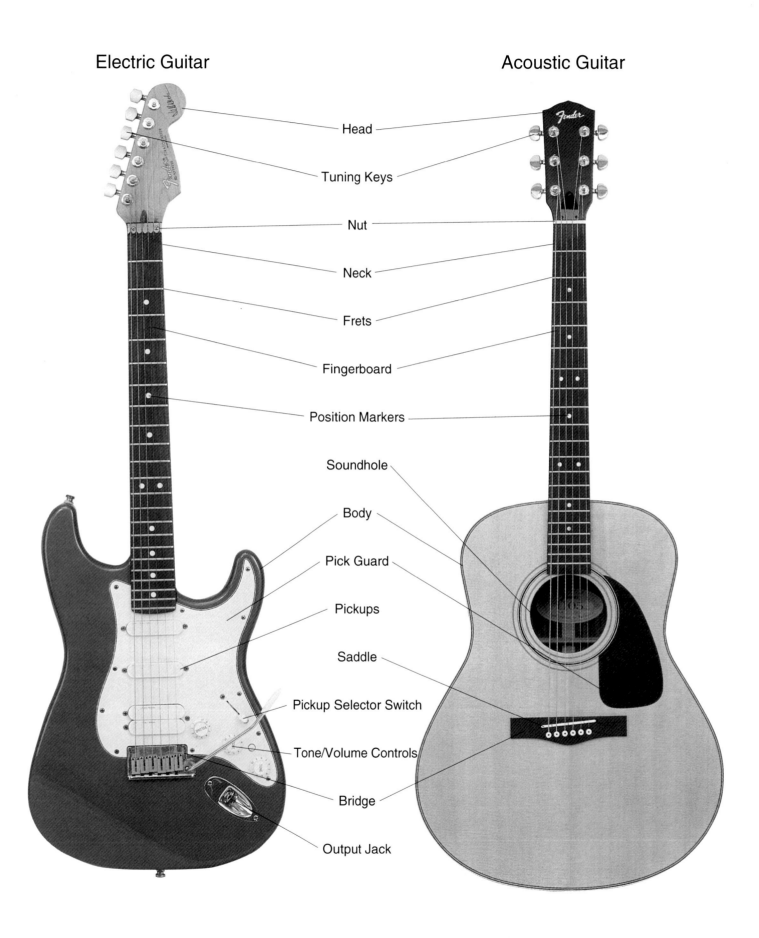

Head

Tuning Keys

Nut

Neck

Frets

Fingerboard

Position Markers

Soundhole

Body

Pick Guard

Pickups

Saddle

Pickup Selector Switch

Tone/Volume Controls

Bridge

Output Jack

Basic Technique

You may play the guitar while either sitting or standing.

Use your left hand to press down notes between the frets. Only the thumb (centered behind the neck) and fingers should touch the neck.

The palm of the picking hand should rest lightly on the bridge with the underside of the forearm resting on the front of the guitar body.

Hold the pick between your thumb and 1st finger and use a downstroke to attack the strings.

◆ Tuning The Guitar

• **W**hen you are tuning the guitar, you will adjust the pitch (highness or lowness of sound) of each string by turning the corresponding tuning key. Tightening a string raises the pitch and loosening it lowers the pitch.

Electronic Guitar Tuner

• If you have an electronic guitar tuner, you can easily tune your guitar by following the instructions that came with the tuner.

Tuning To A Keyboard

• If you have a piano or keyboard, you can easily tune each string as shown:

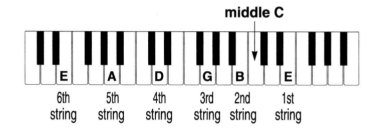

Relative Tuning

To tune your guitar by ear, you must tune the strings to each other. This is done in the following manner:

• Assuming the 6th string is tuned correctly to E, press the 6th string behind the 5th fret, play the depressed 6th string and the open 5th string together. When the two sounds match, you are in tune.

• Press the 5th string behind the 5th fret and tune the open 4th string to it.

• Press the 4th string behind the 5th fret and tune the open 3rd string to it.

• Press the 3rd string behind the 4th fret and tune the open 2nd string to it.

• Press the 2nd string behind the fifth fret and tune the 1st string to it.

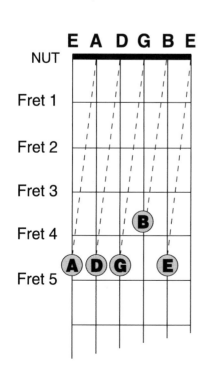

The Musical Staff

Guitar music is notated on a *musical staff*. It shows pitches and rhythm and is divided by bar lines into measures or "bars" of music. The sign at the beginning of the staff is the *treble clef*.

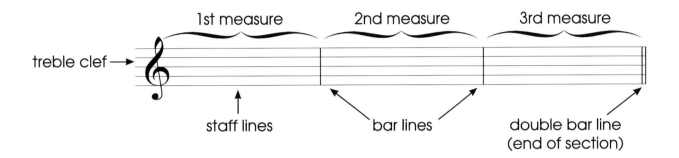

1st measure   2nd measure   3rd measure

treble clef →

staff lines   bar lines   double bar line (end of section)

Each line and space on the staff has a letter name representing a different pitch. Pitches are named from the first seven letters of the alphabet (A, B, C, D, E, F and G).

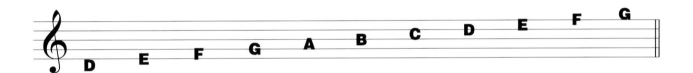

The following tried-and-true tips can be handy in helping you remember the names of the lines and spaces.

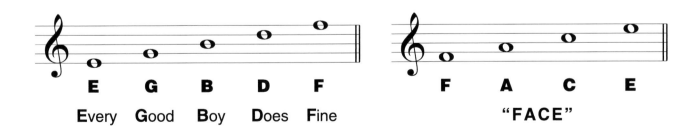

E   G   B   D   F   F   A   C   E

Every Good Boy Does Fine   "FACE"

# The Time Signature

When measures are divided into four, equally-spaced beats, a time signature of "4/4" is used. Four-Four Time means there are four quarter note beats in each measure and is also known as Common Time. Counting "**one**, two, three, four, **one**, two, three, four" with an emphasis on "one" helps us to keep track of the beats and measures.

Time Signature
(Four-Four Time)

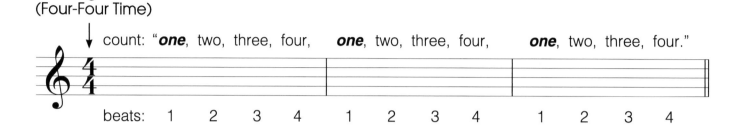

count: "**one**, two, three, four,   **one**, two, three, four,   **one**, two, three, four."

beats: 1   2   3   4   1   2   3   4   1   2   3   4

Rhythm Values And Rests

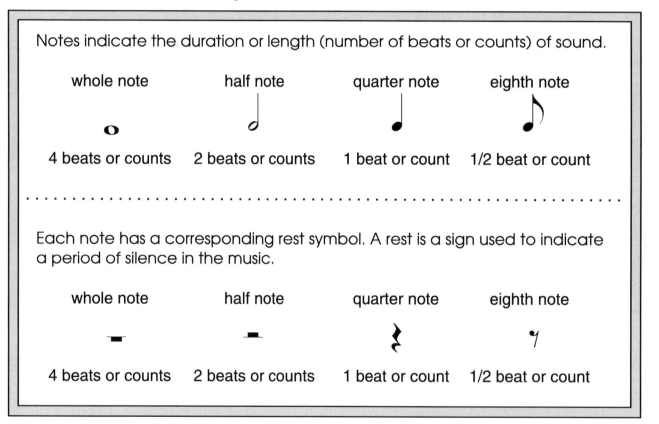

Notes indicate the duration or length (number of beats or counts) of sound.

whole note	half note	quarter note	eighth note
4 beats or counts	2 beats or counts	1 beat or count	1/2 beat or count

Each note has a corresponding rest symbol. A rest is a sign used to indicate a period of silence in the music.

whole note	half note	quarter note	eighth note
4 beats or counts	2 beats or counts	1 beat or count	1/2 beat or count

notes

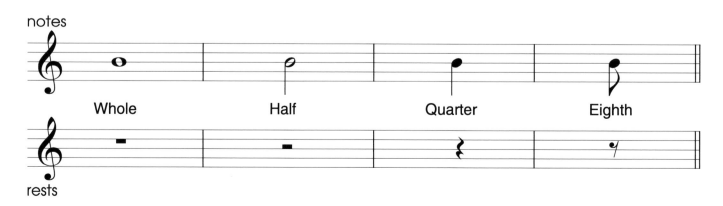

Whole   Half   Quarter   Eighth

rests

The Fingerboard Grid

The fingerboard grid is a handy and useful picture of the fingerboard showing strings, frets and note names.

First, imagine this picture of the fingerboard.

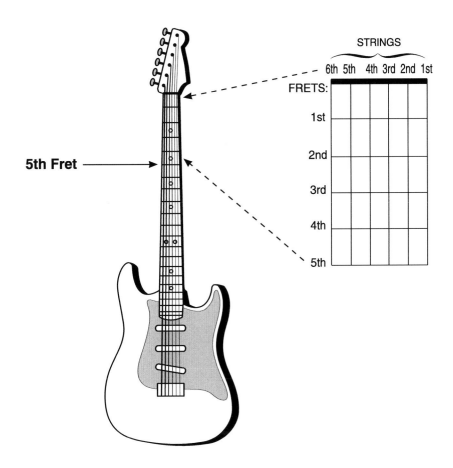

Circles are drawn onto the grid to indicate notes played.

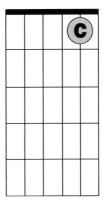

Notes on the 1st String: High E

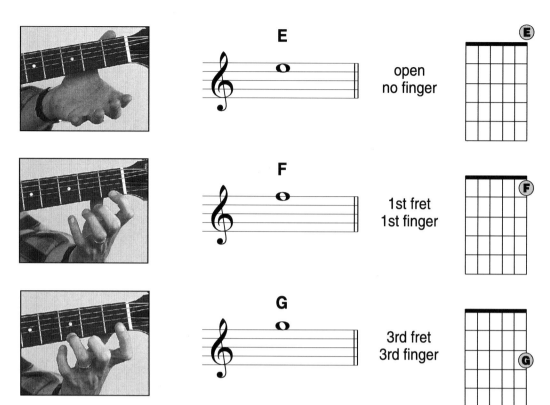

E	open no finger	
F	1st fret 1st finger	
G	3rd fret 3rd finger	

Whole Notes

 = downstroke

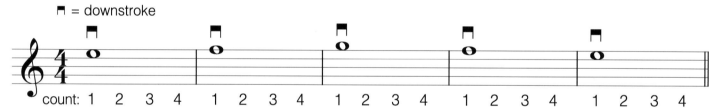

count: 1 2 3 4   1 2 3 4   1 2 3 4   1 2 3 4   1 2 3 4

Half Notes

count: 1 2 3 4   1 2 (3 4)

Quarter Notes

count: 1 2 3 4

1 2 (3 4)

Repeat Signs

Vertical dots before and after a double bar line mean replay the measures enclosed by them. These are called *Repeat Signs.*

Etude 1

Play this twice

Etude 2 ◆4

Etude 3 ◆5

count: 1   2   3   4
    (rest)   (rest)

Notes on the 2nd String: B

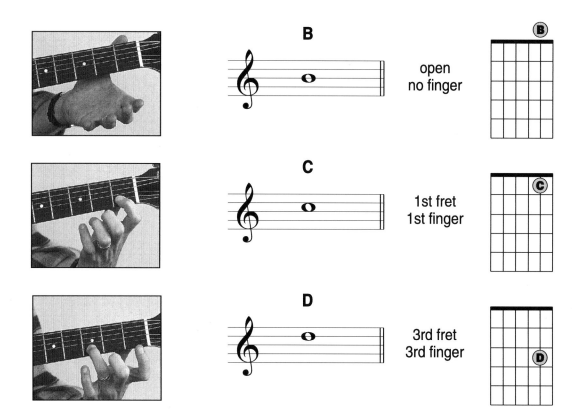

B

open
no finger

C

1st fret
1st finger

D

3rd fret
3rd finger

Whole Notes

(1   2   3   4)

Half Notes

1   2   (3   4)

Dotted Half Note

A dot after a note increases its rhythmic value by one-half. The dotted half note receives three beats.

half note   plus   dot   =   dotted half note
2 beats   plus   1 beat =   3 beats

Etude 4 6

1   2   3   (4)

Etude 5 7

Etude 6 8

Moving between the 1st and 2nd strings:

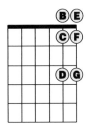

Etude 7 9

Etude 8 10

Etude 9 11

11

◆12 Ode To Joy

Ludwig von Beethoven (1770-1827) was one of the greatest classical composers of all time. The "Ode to Joy" theme is taken from the final movement of his famous 9th Symphony. This beautiful melody has inspired countless composers and musicians.

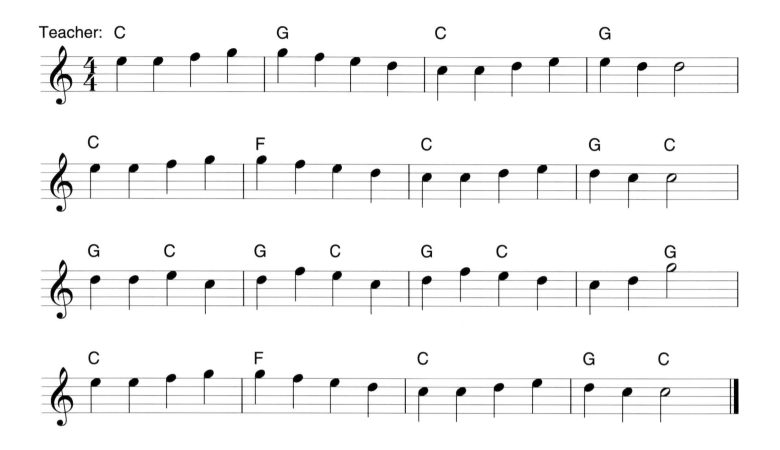

◆13 Au Clair De La Lune

◆14 Kreutzer's Etude #2

Rudolphe Kreutzer (1766-1831) was a genius violinist of the classical and romantic eras. His famed 2nd Etude is a standard in the annals of music. Comedian Jack Benny borrowed it for the theme of his 1950s sitcom and Eddie Van Halen quoted it outright in his famous "Eruption" solo.

Notes On The 3rd String: G

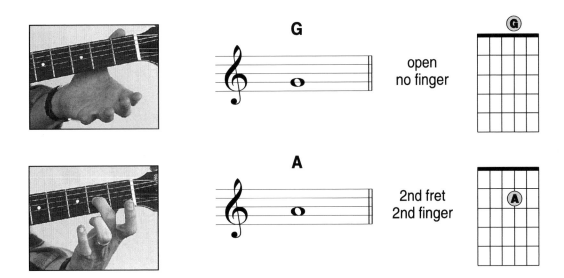

G

open
no finger

A

2nd fret
2nd finger

Etude 10 15

Etude 11 16

Etude 12 17

This melody contains another common melodic pattern. It winds down in a serpentine, ladder-like sort of sequence and makes an ideal daily exercise. You've heard guitarists like Al DiMeola and Yngwie Malmsteem employ these types of lines in their playing.

Etude 13

🔷 Aura Lee

This popular folk melody was revived in the 1950s when it became the source of Elvis Presley's big hit "Love Me Tender." An extremely versatile melody, it was also used as a traditional military song by West Point; appearing then as "Army Blue." The connection between traditional and folk melodies and both pop and classical music is undeniable.

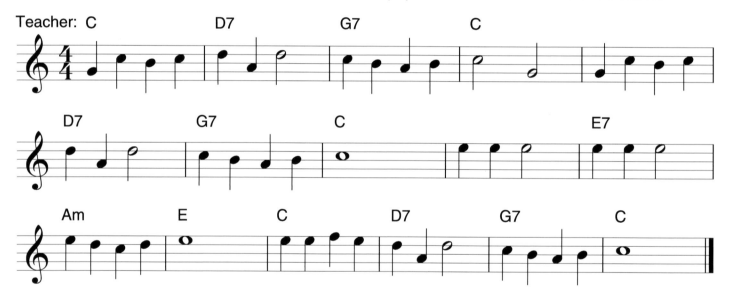

🔷 Blues In G

The blues refers to a Black American song of sorrow which originated in the 1800s as vocal music in the Deep South. Elements of its unique sound can be detected in nearly all forms of modern music, including such guitarists as Muddy Waters, B.B. King, Stevie Ray Vaughan and Eric Clapton.

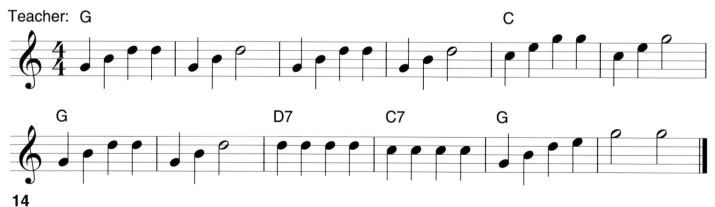

Pick-Up Notes

Music doesn't always begin on the first beat of a measure. When one or more notes occur after beat 1, preceding the beginning of a musical thought or phrase, they are called "pick-up notes."

Here is an example. Count out loud and notice that the first two beats, 1 and 2, are missing from the first measure of the music. You count beats 1 and 2 but actually begin playing on beat three.

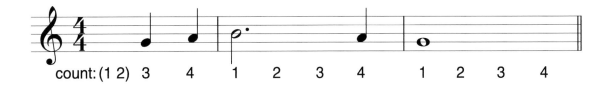

❷❶ Red River Valley

This familiar cowboy tune is another example of a timeless folk melody. It was appropriated in 1959 by the instrumental quintet, Johnny and the Hurricanes, and became the basis of their popular rock and roll hit, "Red River Rock." You've heard this version more recently in the hit comedy film, *Planes, Trains, and Automobiles* starring Steve Martin and John Candy.

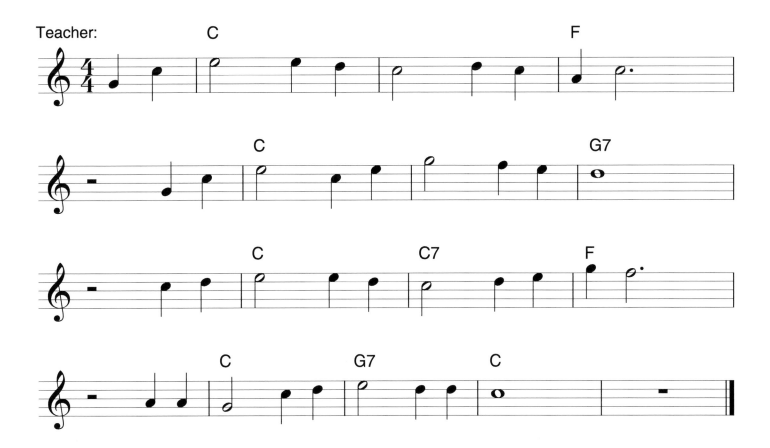

✦22 When The Saints Go Marching In

This well known spiritual was written in 1896 and later became a standard among the New Orleans Dixieland bands. Jazz legend Louis Armstrong enjoyed chart success with his version in 1939 as did the folk group Weavers in 1951.

Three-Four Time

This sign is the time signature for 3/4 time.

3 = 3 beats per measure

4 = a quarter note receives one beat

In 3/4, we have 3 quarter notes per measure. Knowledge and fluency with time signatures is vital to all musicians. Metal bands like Metallica and Megadeth use all sorts of unusual and changing meters to give their songs a unique rhythmic energy while the waltz and gigue are staples of classical and traditional dance music.

✦23 Drink To Me Only With Thine Eyes

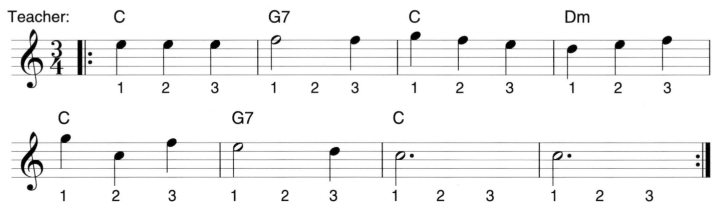

Notes On The 4th String: D

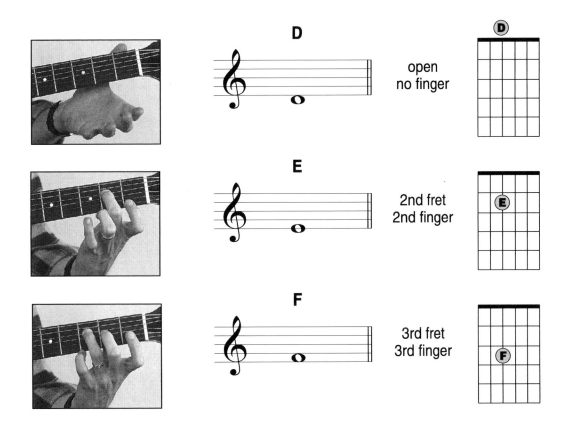

Etude 14 24

Etude 15 (The Snake Charmer) 25

26 The Battle Hymn Of The Republic

The origin of this patriotic melody dates back to the mid-1800s known then as "Glory Hallelujah." It has since entered the charts six times (including Elvis' live medley rendition) and continues to remain a staple in traditional repertoire.

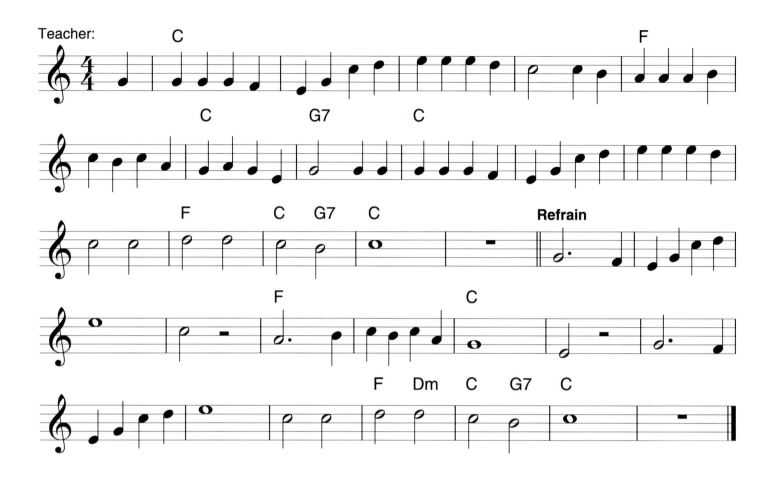

27 Cielito Lindo

This Mexican folk song was popularly revived in 1923 with the lyrics "Ay, Ay, Ay, Ay." You may also have heard Ricky Ricardo sing it on the television show *I Love Lucy*.

Eighth Notes

An eighth note () is half the length of a quarter note. It receives one-half beat in 4/4 or 3/4 time.

Two or more successive eighth notes are usually connected by a beam.

Two eighth notes equal one quarter note.

Etude 16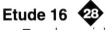

= downpick

count: 1 and 2 and 3 and 4 and

Next let's convert a couple of our previously-played melodies to an eighth note rhythm format.

Kreutzer's Etude #2 29

Etude 17 (The Snake Charmer) 30

Ties

An arched line which connects two (or more) successive notes of the same pitch is called a "tie." The first note of the tie is struck but the next is (are) not.
It is (they are) added to the time value of the first.

In this example, a half note is tied to a dotted half note. A half is worth two beats and a dotted half is worth three, so the total duration of time is five beats.
Strike it once but hold it for five counts.

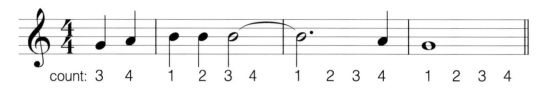

◆31 Amazing Grace

Gospel music is at the very roots of rock, blues, folk and pop styles. "Amazing Grace" is an all-time favorite, inspiring R&B artists like Ray Charles as well as folk singers such as Judy Collins, who had a top 40 hit with it in 1971. Modern rock guitarist Steve Vai came up with his own version of the song in the soundtrack of the movie, *Dudes.*

◆32 Down In The Valley

◆ Midnight Special

This tune is a standard in country rock and pop genres. Both Paul Evans and Johnny Rivers had top 20 hits with it in the 1960s and virtuoso picker Albert Lee recently recorded a swinging rockabilly rendition.

Notes On The 5th String: A

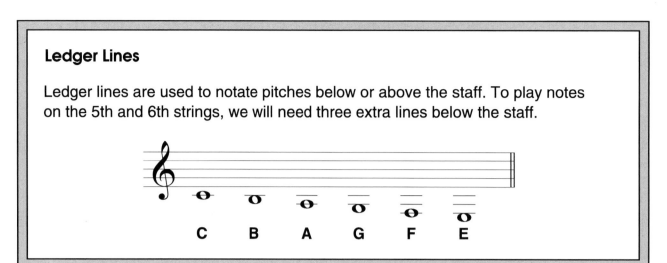

Ledger Lines

Ledger lines are used to notate pitches below or above the staff. To play notes on the 5th and 6th strings, we will need three extra lines below the staff.

C   B   A   G   F   E

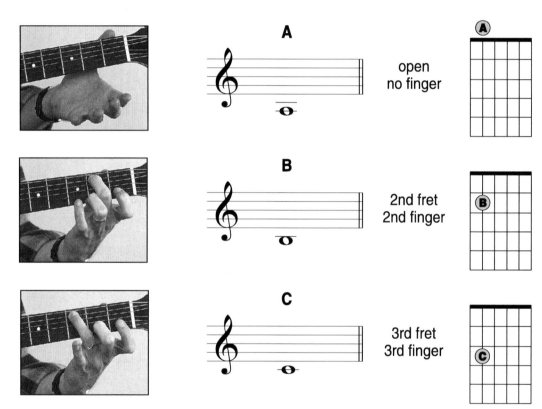

A

open
no finger

B

2nd fret
2nd finger

C

3rd fret
3rd finger

Etude 18 🔶34

Etude 19 🔶35

◆36◆ House Of The Rising Sun

This haunting blues-inspired song became the basis for the Animals' first big rock hit in the mid-1960s.

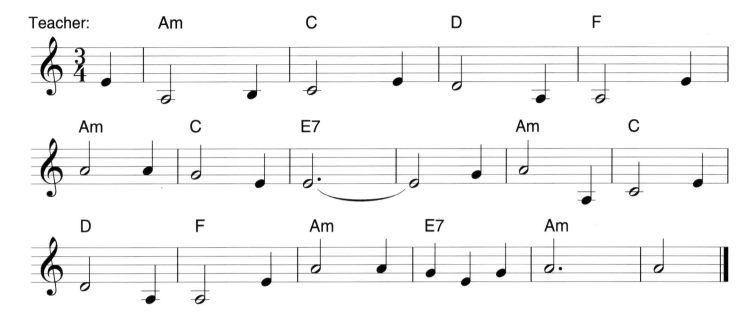

◆37◆ Greensleeves

King Henry VIII is credited as the true author of this beautiful English traditional, written sometime in the 16th century. Guitarist Jeff Beck rendered a lovely acoustic version on his classic 1968 album, *Truth*.

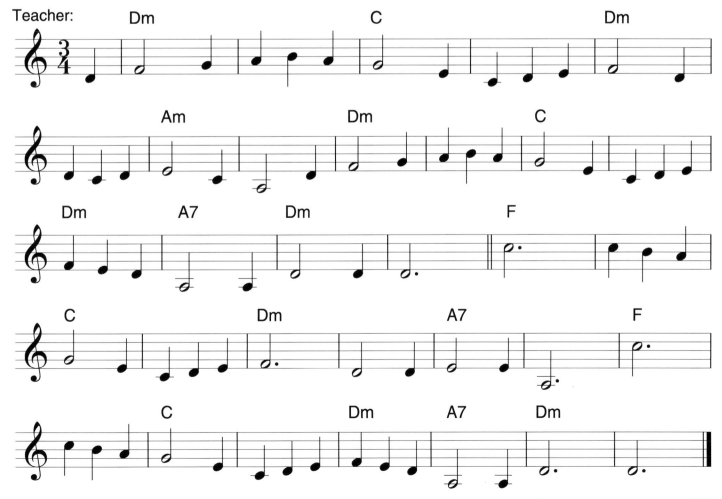

◆38 Rockin' Riff

The riff, a slang term originating from the words "repeated figure," is a central principle in rock, blues, country and pop music. Many tunes are remembered largely by their signature riff.

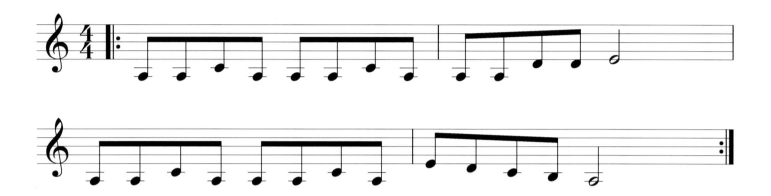

◆39 Beethoven's 5th Symphony (1st Theme)

This familiar Beethoven melody from his 5th Symphony is an immortal theme which received many pop and rock versions including Walter Murphy's disco track "A Fifth of Beethoven" and Yngwie Malmsteen's powerful neo-classic metal rendition on his *Live in Leningrad* album.

Notes On The 6th String: Low E

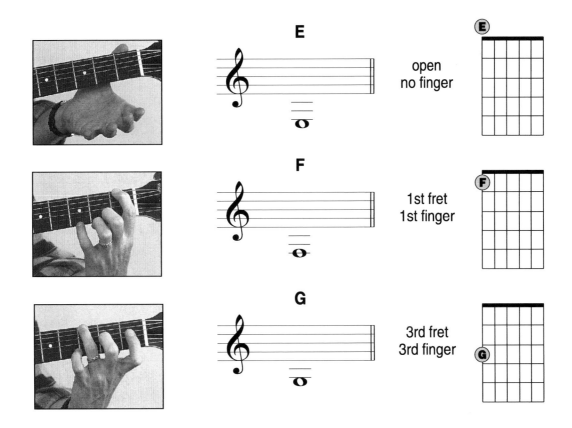

E

open
no finger

F

1st fret
1st finger

G

3rd fret
3rd finger

The notes on the low E, 6th string, are identical in shape to the notes on the high E, 1st string. The pitch names are also the same.

Etude 20 40

Etude 21 41

42 Johnny Has Gone For A Soldier

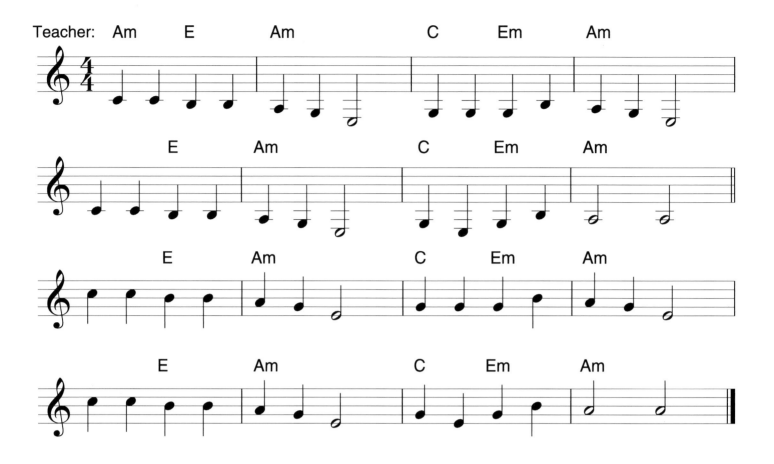

43 Sailors Hornpipe

This comic tune is a great workout in eighth notes. It's a popular folk melody found in bluegrass playoffs and country picking contests and is familiar to most as the "Popeye" theme.

The Eighth Rest

This is an eighth rest:

It represent one-half beat of silence in 4/4 or 3/4 time.

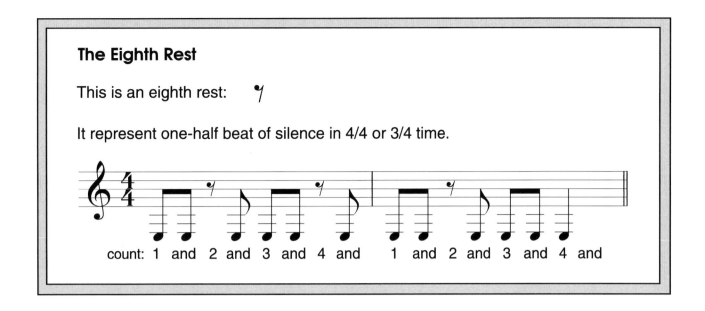

count: 1 and 2 and 3 and 4 and   1 and 2 and 3 and 4 and

◆44 Shenandoah

This melodious folk tune was once recorded by jazz guitarist Johnny Smith.

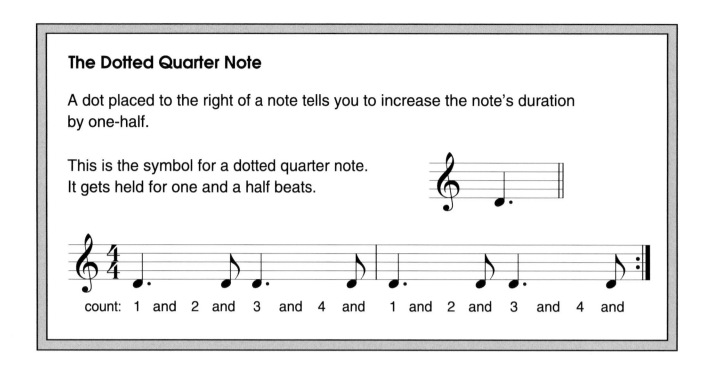

The Dotted Quarter Note

A dot placed to the right of a note tells you to increase the note's duration by one-half.

This is the symbol for a dotted quarter note.
It gets held for one and a half beats.

count: 1 and 2 and 3 and 4 and 1 and 2 and 3 and 4 and

Here's a riff on the lowest two strings using a dotted quarter note rhythm.

Etude 22 45

46 Rockabilly Riff

Teacher: G

C   G

D   C   G

◆47 Scarborough Fair

The pop/folk rock duo Simon and Garfunkel enjoyed a huge late-1960s hit with their memorable rendition of this immortal folk tune.

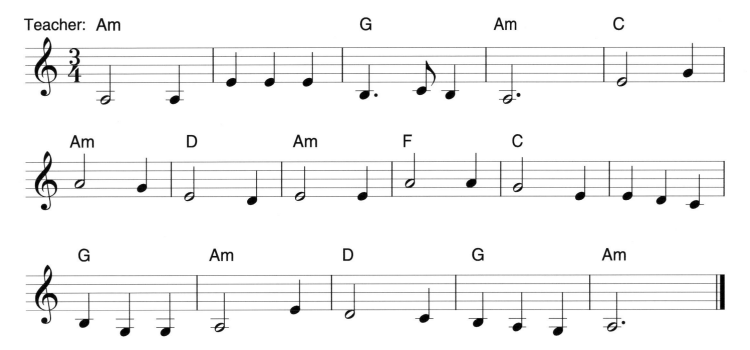

◆48 Swing Low, Sweet Chariot

"Swing Low, Sweet Chariot" is a classic gospel tune which has inspired countless R&B, pop and blues musicians. It uses dotted quarter note rhythms and notes on the low E string.

Sixteenth Notes

A sixteenth note is worth half of an eighth note or one quarter of a beat. It may appear alone with a solid notehead, stem and two flags;

or in groups of two or more with two beams.

In 4/4 time, sixteenth notes subdivide each beat into four parts and each measure into 16 (hence sixteenth note) parts.

When playing sixteenth notes, we use alternate picking. This involves alternating between downstrokes (∨) and upstrokes ( ).

🔶49 Eine Kleine Nachtmusik
(A Little Night Music)

Now let's apply 16th notes to our playing. Be sure to use alternate picking when playing the sixteenth notes in the third line. Here's a classic theme from Mozart.

The High A Note

A

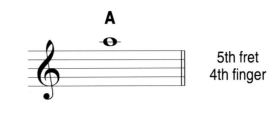

5th fret
4th finger

Etude 23 50

Etude 24 51

52 Auld Lang Syne